50 Things to Know

50 THINGS TO KNOW ABOUT BEING IN THE PEACE CORPS

Spreading the Peace

Margo Willis

50 Things to Know About Being in the Peace Corps Copyright © 2021 by CZYK Publishing LLC.
All Rights Reserved.

All rights reserved. No part of this book may be reproduced in any form or by any electronic or mechanical means including information storage and retrieval systems, without permission in writing from the author. The only exception is by a reviewer, who may quote short excerpts in a review.
The statements in this book are of the authors and may not be the views of CZYK Publishing or 50 Things to Know.

Cover designed by: Ivana Stamenkovic
Cover Image:
https://en.wikipedia.org/wiki/Peace_Corps#/media/File:Peace_corps_logo16.svg

CZYK Publishing Since 2011.
CZYKPublishing.com
50 Things to Know

Lock Haven, PA
All rights reserved.

ISBN: 9798738513350

50 THINGS TO KNOW BOOK SERIES REVIEWS FROM READERS

I recently downloaded a couple of books from this series to read over the weekend thinking I would read just one or two. However, I so loved the books that I read all the six books I had downloaded in one go and ended up downloading a few more today. Written by different authors, the books offer practical advice on how you can perform or achieve certain goals in life, which in this case is how to have a better life.

The information is simple to digest and learn from, and is incredibly useful. There are also resources listed at the end of the book that you can use to get more information.

50 Things To Know To Have A Better Life: Self-Improvement Made Easy!

Author Dannii Cohen

This book is very helpful and provides simple tips on how to improve your everyday life. I found it to be useful in improving my overall attitude.

50 Things to Know For Your Mindfulness & Meditation Journey
Author Nina Edmondso

Quick read with 50 short and easy tips for what to think about before starting to homeschool.

50 Things to Know About Getting Started with Homeschool by Author Amanda Walton

I really enjoyed the voice of the narrator, she speaks in a soothing tone. The book is a really great reminder of things we might have known we could do during stressful times, but forgot over the years.

Author Harmony Hawaii

There is so much waste in our society today. Everyone should be forced to read this book. I know I am passing it on to my family.

50 Things to Know to Downsize Your Life: How To Downsize, Organize, And Get Back to Basics

Author Lisa Rusczyk Ed. D.

Great book to get you motivated and understand why you may be losing motivation. Great for that person who wants to start getting healthy, or just for you when you need motivation while having an established workout routine.

50 Things To Know To Stick With A Workout: Motivational Tips To Start The New You Today

Author Sarah Hughes

50 THINGS TO KNOW ABOUT BEING IN THE PEACE CORPS

BOOK DESCRIPTION

Do you want a job that can make a difference? Do you like to travel and see the world? Do you want a job that presents a challenge and pushes you outside your zone? Have you thought about joining the Peace Corps? If you answered yes to any of these questions, then this book is for you...

50 Things to Know About Being in the Peace Corps by author Margo Willis offers an approach to the ins and outs of the Peace Corps. Most books on The Peace Corps tell you the basics of what is like to be in the Peace Corps. Although there's nothing wrong with that, the Peace Corps is so much more than that. Every one's experience is slightly different from another's, my hope is to be able to condense all the information I know about the Peace Corps so that people can make informed decisions on whether or not the Peace Corps is right for you.

In these pages you'll discover the good, the bad, and the ugly aspects of volunteering in the Peace Corps. This book will help you make the choice on whether service is the right option for you!

By the time you finish this book, you will know what it's like to service, how the Peace Corps is run in the countries that are served, and the benefits and disadvantages to service as well. So grab YOUR copy today. You'll be glad you did.

TABLE OF CONTENTS

50 Things to Know
Book Series
Reviews from Readers
50 Things to Know About Being in the Peace Corps
BOOK DESCRIPTION
TABLE OF CONTENTS
DEDICATION
ABOUT THE AUTHOR
INTRODUCTION
1. Go in Blind
2. Preparing to Leave
3. Arriving in Country
4. First Two Months are a Whirlwind
5. Training, Training, Training
6. Set Up for Success
7. Everything is Provided for you
8. Learning New Skills
9. PACA
10. Weird Modes of Transportation
11. Safety and Security
12. PCMO
13. Travel
14. Lots of Free Time
15. Get Out What You Put in

16. Counterparts
17. Isolation
18. Keeping connected
19. Mail
20. All Eyes on You
21. Questions, T.V Stereotypes
22. New Family
23. New Community
24. Culture Shock
25. Home Sickness
26. Traveling to the Capital
27. Getting Sick
28. Flexibility
29. Integration.
30. Friendships
31. Making Small Differences
32. Conversions
33. Navigating Gender and Societal Roles and Norms
34. Reporting
35. Acronyms
36. Personal Space
37. Language Barriers
38. Money
39. It's All About the Small Things in Life
40. Third World Problems

41. Overwhelming
42. Holidays
43. Talk to a recruiter before leaving
44. Everyone's Service is Difference 6
45. Sense of Purpose
46. Change of Perspective
47. Opportunities
48. Evacuation
49. Non-Competitive Eligibility
50. Reintegration

Other Resources:
50 Things to Know

DEDICATION

I would like to thank my dad who has always been supportive in everything I have done and continue to do.

ABOUT THE AUTHOR

I grew up in Harpers Ferry West Virginia and went to University close to home where I studied Sociology with a minor in Spanish. I joined the Peace Corps shortly after I graduated in an attempt to buy time to figure out what to do next as well as a desire for adventure. I served in Ukraine I a small village along the Ukrainian, Romanian boarder. I also wanted the opportunity to Travel which I love to do. In my free time I also like to read and write.

I am currently serving as an AmeriCorps Vista member in southern Arizona, working with a non-profit as a family enrichment specialist. I live in Eloy Arizona with my cat and do my best to serve my community as much as I possibly can.

I can be found on Instagram at rainstraveldiary_97

INTRODUCTION

"But if the life will not be easy, it will be rich and satisfying. For every young American who participates in the Peace's Corps – who works in a foreign land will know that her or she is sharing the in the greatest common task of bringing man that decent way of life which is the foundation of freedom and a condition of peace."

John F Kennedy.

The Peace Corps was created by President John. F. Kennedy in the March of 1961, when two students at the University of Michigan gave him the idea during his election tour. In September of 1961, the Peace Corps was put into an Act by Congress making the Peace Corps a branch of the State Department a few years later. 60 years later Peace Corps serves 61 countries with over 7,000 volunteers on the front lines. The Peace Corps has three primary goals the first one is sector specific, the second is sharing American Culture with your host country, and the third is sharing your host country's culture with Americans that you meet. Overall, I think Peace Corps service is an amazing opportunity for those who desire adventure and want to challenge themselves. It has been said that the Peace Corps is the hardest job that you will ever love, and I whole heartedly think that is true.

This is my own personal view on what I have experienced, I am not a recruiter and what follows is in now way a direct reflection of the views of the Peace Corps in General.

1. GO IN BLIND

Joining the Peace Corps is a big leap of faith, so it is only natural to research as much as possible. It is probably why you are reading this book right now, and although research is important, I recommend keeping an open mind. First of all, everyone's service is different, there will be somethings you w/on't expected. Secondly keeping a bit of mystery about the country you are going to serve will help you keep an open mind. I went into service knowing very little which I am glad I did, because it made my service a lot easier to manage. It also made my own service more interesting not knowing exactly what was right around the corner. I knew very little about Ukraine, but throughout the course of my service I learned so much through the connections I made which was very important to me personally. Now I am not saying to not do research at all, you wouldn't read this book otherwise. The next 49 tips consist of the things that I feel should be known before going into this experience, so I recommend leaving somethings to the imagination for right now. I promise you'll find out soon enough!

2. PREPARING TO LEAVE

Leaving your whole life behind can be a bit overwhelming and fitting your whole life in just a few small bags can be challenging. It will be one of the many challenges that you will face throughout the term of your Peace Corps service. At least for me the Peace Corps sent a list of recommended items to bring and for the most part I brought what I could. That being said I was only limited to two 50 pounds bags and a carry on and personal item. For those who chose to go to warmer countries than the one I served in, you will only be allowed to bring one 50-pound bag, plus your carry on and personal item. I suggest you start with the basics and think whether or not you actually need an item. Choose what you bring carefully, and keep in mind that most things can be bought in the capital shortly after your arrival. I would also suggest bringing something of comfort, and something that reminds you of home, because more likely than not you will experience homesickness at some point throughout your service. I would also recommend bringing spices that you love because there is a high chance you will not be able to find them in your country of service.

3. ARRIVING IN COUNTRY

I served in Eastern Europe, so I had a long journey to arrive to my country of Service. I went from L.A to Kyiv Ukraine in a matter of 48 hours, and it was a really long trip. The flight itself with a layover took over ten hours, not including the time it took for the group of 54 people to check into the flight and board the plane. Arriving in Ukraine for the first time was very exciting, and there were both

Peace Corps Volunteers and Host Country Nationals were there to greet us as well. Once Arriving in country, we boarded a bus and was carted to a hotel where we would be staying for the next few days for training and sort of a meet and greet with staff and the other volunteers that came with you. I recommend you use this time to meet people and develop connections because these connections could help make or break your experience with the Peace Corps. All the staff I meet at the Peace Corps were super friendly and they will support you as best as they can. I would also recommend for the first week there and well for the rest of service, just go with a flow. I say this because at first it may seem kind of hectic, but I promise you there is a method to the madness.

4. FIRST TWO MONTHS ARE A WHIRLWIND

Each Country runs there trainings slightly different, based off of many different factors, including, finances, resources, and sector in which you are serving in. For me Personally I was a TEFL volunteer which stands for Teaching English as a Second Language. After my first week at the hotel, after being put into small groups, we were sent to sites a few hours away from the capital city for training along with our small groups. At the training sites we were set up with a host family (a family that would give you a place to stay and give you food, support, ect), and we began training. My group spent 4 hours-5 hours a day, 5 days a week specifically on learning the language. The other time was spent learning other skills you would need to learn in order to thrive at your new job and the responsibilities you would soon take on. My recommendation for you, is to take advantage of this training, particularly the language learning because it will help you through out the two years you are there. Also take time for self-care when you can because the first two months are a lot, and it is very easy to become overwhelmed. It will fly by faster than you will realize.

5. TRAINING, TRAINING, TRAINING

There is a high chance that there will be trainings through out your term of service, even after you have given your oath of service. I can't say for certain the types of training you will receive, but I can tell you what I experienced. Training was always fun, because it was a time to get together with the friends you made through the first two months of your training. Training is a good time to meet with friends and get to know your counterpart. I highly recommend that you take this time to really get to know your counterpart because they oftentimes participate in the training with you, and you will be spending a long amount of time traveling together. Lastly training is a great way to get out of your site and get a break for about a week.

6. SET UP FOR SUCCESS

The Peace Corps is putting a lot on the line and trust in you as an individual to send you to another country. That's why they are going to do their best to help you succeed. I personally went in with no knowledge of teaching myself, and they gave me the tools I needed to be a successful teacher. First of all they used the same teaching techniques they wanted us to use to teach English in everything they taught us from Language to so much more. This was very helpful because it showed us what exactly they were expecting from us, despite that the trainings would seem childish at some points in time. I can't say for sure whether the other sectors do the same thing, but I do imagine that they do. My advice would be to take this all in and use it to be successful in your job, and please do not write it off as childish. It is very beneficial

7. EVERYTHING IS PROVIDED FOR YOU

Perhaps one of the best things that I appreciated about being in the Peace Corps is that I really didn't have to worry about much. Going to a new country where you are not familiar with what is like is intimidating, especially if you are unfamiliar with the language to begin with. Peace Corps staff in country work with your villages to make sure that there will be acceptable living situations. There is a high chance you will be placed into a Host family when you arrive to your site at least for the first three months. Then you can either stay with your host family or work with your counterpart to find an independent living situation. For me I was placed into both, so I really didn't have to worry about where to live. You will also be provided the funds to be able to buy food and housing for yourself, plus a little extra if you use it wisely. Any medications you need will also be provided by Peace Corps Medical Office, so you won't have to worry about that as well. I suggest that if you spend your money wisely you will do quite well for yourself.

8. LEARNING NEW SKILLS

Peace Corps Service can often be complex and can change based off of the village you serve and many other factors as well. The Peace Corps will have training that will help you in many aspects of your service both personally or professionally. An example of such is a training I took in Project Management in Design, despite the fact that My sector was TEFL (Teaching English as a Foreign Language). I also had the opportunity to take training in PEPFAR (Presidential Emergency Plan for AIDs relief. I also know someone who served in Gana and he took training in Malaria prevention. I think these trainings are a great opportunity and look great on a resume, so I suggest you participate where you can. Plus, these trainings are an excuse to travel from your site, which can be a nice break.

9. PACA

A good portion of my training was studying and getting familiar with PACA stands for the Participatory Approach to Community Action, and you will hear it a lot through out your Peace Corps service. PACA is a guide designed specifically for Peace Corps and it is a guide for developing projects within your community. It is the slight touch on to Project Management and Design 90. Although PACA can be kind of boring and self-explanatory at times, I suggest that you get accustom to the tools that it provides. The tools could definitely help you throughout your service, especially if you are in a more project centered sector like Youth Development.

10. WEIRD MODES OF TRANSPORTATION

You will be living in a third world country, but of course you already knew that. Most likely you will have to travel by bus, or train. For me I traveled by both, each a different experience. The bus in Ukraine is called a Marshrutka, and they aren't the best mode of transportation. More often than not they were busy and very hot in the summer. I would recommend bringing a good set of headphones and bring something you can use to play music. It may also be beneficial to have music predownloaded on whatever device you plan to bring, because there is a high likelihood that you will not always have the ability to play music off of Spotify or Pandora. Music isn't a must if there is something small you can bring to occupy your time, I suggest bringing that too, if you think you can. Also, try and tra3vel with a buddy at all possible. This will A help secure both of your safety and B. gives you someone to talk to.

11. SAFETY AND SECURITY

When you go into the Peace Corps and you arrive at your country of service, they take steps to ensure that you are safe. That is the job for the Safety Security team that is stationed at your country of service. During your first few weeks they will explain many things to you including the evacuation plan in case anything was to happen. They also have guidelines they will follow when you go and move into an independent living situation. Part of their job as well is to make sure the site you will be] living in is safe. I suggest you listen to there advise, more often than not the safety security team will be comprised of Host Country National who will know the safety risks of their given country, and are the best equip to tell you how to keep yourself safe during your service.

12. PCMO

Peace Corps Medical Office will do whatever they can to help full fill your medical needs, including providing medicine and doctors visits when need be. Usually the Medical office is stationed in the capital city where the Peace Corps Country Office is, so to see the doctors on staff and to receive medication be aware you will have to travel to the capital city. My recommendation is to try and schedule med pick ups when you know you need to be in the capital for stuff like training. Also do your best to plan as far out ahead as you possibly can because travel can be time consuming depending on where you are stationed and the country in which you are living.

13. TRAVEL

Travel is one of the many benefits of Peace Corps Service. One of the things I recommend is to save as much money as you can so you can travel on your free time. You probably won't need much because there is a high chance that travelling will not cost as much as it would have originally cost to travel from the United States. Also keep close attention where you keep your passport because it is very important that you have it with you when you travel as well as whatever documentation the country you live in may give you. I also highly recommend you plan vacations from time to time and get away. Everyone needs a break, and take this opportunity to see things you may have never been able to see otherwise.

14. LOTS OF FREE TIME

Once training is over and you go to your site, you will find that you will have a lot of free time on your hands. For example, in my sector I would spend 20 hours a week doing my actual job, that rounded out to working 4 days a week at about 6 hours each day, the shift from constantly being busy during training to cutting those hours nearly in half was mind boggling, and at first I didn't know what to exactly do with my time. My recommendation for this is to use this time to learn a new skill. Many people I knew in the Peace Corps learned to cook, knit, and or sew, just to name a few. Personally, I spent a lot of my free time reading and listening to audiobooks, as well as studying the language.

15. GET OUT WHAT YOU PUT IN

Like mentioned earlier, you have a lot of free time, and you can choose how to spend your free time. That being said, you have a lot of autonomy which can be both good and bad. Pretty much what you gain from the Peace Corps will be as much as you are willing to put in. I recommend using your free time to start a secondary project within the community. Get to know the people in your community and spend time with the people you work with as much as possible. You can learn so much by interacting with the people in your community, including but not limited to language and culture. My host mom in particular taught me so much including, how to fold laundry, how to cook traditional meals, and I also taught her how to cook some American dishes like pancakes.

16. COUNTERPARTS

Part of the goal of Peace Corps is sustainability, and in order to help the community you serve to help themselves the Peace Corps pairs you with a counterpart. To put it simply your job is not to build a well for your community but to show your community how to build a well so they can continue to build wells after you are gone. Counterparts are an important part of your service; they are most likely the person you go to if you need anything while at site. Not all counterparts are created equal but do your best to develop a good connection with your counterpart. A good counterpart-volunteer connection could make or break your service.

17. ISOLATION

There is a high chance that you will be spending most of your time away from other volunteers. The likely hood of more than one volunteer serving in the same city or town is very slim. There is also the fact as mentioned that travel isn't as easy to come by usually as it is in the United States, you really have to plan your trips in coordination with a bus schedule that can at times be finicky. Do not let that dissuade you from travel though, try to make time to hang out with your fellow Peace Corps volunteers, it As well as everyone who is in charge of you could potentially live hours away from you. This job is perfect if you are an independent worker, however its ok to email higher ups if you have questions. I also recommend that you try and make time to hang out with other volunteers from time to time.

18. KEEPING CONNECTED

Often times it is hard to stay connected with friends and family back home when you are living in another country. There are apps on your phone that you can download and have your friends and family download before your service. These apps include but not limited to, whatsup app, telegram, and Viber. Although those apps are great, I suggest keeping in contact with Facebook messenger, I feel like it is easier because more people have Facebook than any of the other apps and the likelihood of reaching someone is higher. The Peace Corps will most likely provide you with a phone and a phone number, however long-distance phone calls can be expensive and can come out of your pocket, eventually. Having a social media account like Facebook and Instagram is a great way to keep connected

19. MAIL

Oftentimes how mail works can vary from country to country. This is something I recommend looking into before your service because chances are, you are probably going to want to receive care packages. If you live in Europe, Asia, or Africa, there is a likelihood that mail could take up to a month to reach to you. How mail worked in Ukraine was that a package would be shipped to the post office where I would have to go to pick it up. Although I don't know for sure, I have a feeling that most Third World Countries operate in a similar fashion. Also note that you will not be able to receive packages during your training period. During my Peace Corps service I especially got excited when I got a package or a letter it showed that my family was thinking about me and oftentimes was the highlight of that day.

20. ALL EYES ON YOU

Often times you are the first American many of these people have met. People are going to want to take there phot with you or talk with you as if you were a celebrity, because to them you kind of are. Everyone will be watching you, but don't let that dishearten you or dissuade you from service. Although there are times where this attention can become uncomfortable and sometimes it can cross the line into the stalker area (talk to counter part and safety and security if this ever happens) don't read too much into it. I recommend baring with the photos and conversations for the most part it will make your community really happy. There is also the fact that you more likely than not will be living in a small town, and word about what you say or do will spread really fast. This phenomenon that you will experience throughout your Peace Corps service can also come in handy at times because there will be times where people will want to give you things like food and clothes, which would make my day when that happened.

21. QUESTIONS, T.V STEREOTYPES

Like mentioned earlier people have probably never seen an American in person. Their only sense of American culture and behavior are from television. Of course, they are going to be curious, and they are going to ask a lot of questions, some of which may seem ridiculous. My host mom would ask whether or not it is snowing in America, which to me seemed kind of strange. They will also assume that you are rich, even though you and your family may not be. I have a friend, who served in Ghana, and he told me a story of how he had to buy nets in order to teach malaria prevention. He talked to a merchant who was selling the nets already knowing what the price would be, and low and behold my friend was told a completely different price much higher than what he was expecting. It's hard for people to understand others from another culture, but there are tons of people willing to try so take this time to teach them what American culture truly is and how vast it can be as well.

22. NEW FAMILY

When you move to your host country, more likely than not you will be placed with a host family to begin with. I was placed into two homes, one during training and one when I was placed in my village. For me, the families I was placed with were very loving, treating me as if I were their own daughter. I recommend learning their customs, make time to actually sit down and spend with your family, because here is where you are going to learn the most a bout the culture of your new home. For me personally I spent a lot of time with my host mom in the kitchen learning to cook. My host family would also invite me to picnic and gatherings with their friends, which was a great gateway into the community which is an integral part of your Peace Corps Service. Personally, the time spent with my host family was probably the highlight of my service and although I was nervous at first, they turned out to be really nice and an integral part of my service

23. NEW COMMUNITY

One of the great things about Peace Corps service was the sense of community that was brought along with it. I'm not only speaking about the host community that you were placed along side with, but also the community of Peace Corps volunteers that are sent along side you. I felt enveloped into a whole new Peace Corps community that was supportive and great the second I walked off the plane at LAX. Other Peace Corps volunteers were waiting to great us when I got off the plane in Kyiv, and immediately I was enveloped into many Peace Corps Facebook groups, and was incorporated into the Returned Peace Corps Volunteer Community on Facebook and in a city close by my hometown. There is something about shared experiences that can bring people together, and Peace Corps is a huge community with one solitary experience that can last a lifetime. Embracing this community can have many added benefits both during your service and after. Use the community for what its worth, ask questions, offer social/emotional support to other Peace Corps Volunteers, and allow yourself to be supported as well by this community.

24. CULTURE SHOCK

The cultures in which the Peace Corps serves can be vast and varied, which can be a lot to take in at times. At first during training, you are so busy that you hardly have the time to miss home, and at least I was still caught in that honeymoon phase. For me Culture Shock came in small things and really makes you grateful that you live in a first world culture. I dealt with the culture shook by reading and listening to audiobooks, just to have a piece of America at my fingertips when I really needed it. A lot of people also listened to music and watch movies and YouTube videos. Another thing that helps with culture shock is sharing your culture with those you are near. I did this by sharing American Holidays, Movies and Music. I also had the ability to make Thanksgiving dinner for my host family, and their extended family which was really nice, and I know my host family appreciated it as well. I also recommend making time to keep in contact with your family and friends.

25. HOME SICKNESS

As mentioned earlier, home sickness is almost bound to happen, some more than others. For me I really started to feel homesick when I wasn't as busy, so one of the things I did was to keep myself busy with whatever I could. Spending time with my counterparts, my host family and other Peace Corps volunteers helped. The holidays were also the worst, so I was grateful when I had the opportunity to meet up with other Peace Corps Volunteers to celebrate some of the important holidays like Thanksgiving, and Christmas. I was fortunate to live in an area where the other Peace Corps volunteers within a relatively short traveling distance from me were really close, it made the holidays a little easier to bare as we met up and spent the holidays together. Requesting letters and the occasional care package from home also helps if you have the ability to do so. I recommend bringing photos of home, and other things you might miss like peanut butter, hot sauce and other spices you love.

26. TRAVELING TO THE CAPITAL

Traveling to the capital city is always a treat. Here is where you may be able to find some things you may not find in your village, like restaurants and other delicacies. For me the capital city was always a place to eat at a restaurant and go to buy things you normally can't otherwise like spices and supplies. Traveling to the capital is also a good place to meet up with other Peace Corps volunteers and is also where you usually go for your training and anything else you might need for Medical, and any paperwork that is needed. There will be opportunities to go to the Capital city and I recommend using this time wisely by scheduling your trips with other Peace Corps Volunteers. Enjoy this time, it is always great to be able to get out and visit the Capital.

27. GETTING SICK

There is a high chance that you will get sick and being sick in a place that isn't your home can be really uncomfortable. Good thing is that the Peace Corps Medical Office gives all the things that you need. At the beginning of your service, you will be handed a big box full of medicines like ibuprofen and pepmo bismal which is a god send. They give you medication, because they have to cooperate with FDA guidelines while you are there, and most likely than not most medication you can find do not have FDA approval. Take the time you need off and get some rest and ask the Peace Corps Medical Office for anything you might need. Also in the beginning the Peace Corps Medical Office will give a rundown on the medical dangers in your given country. Listen to them, they know what they are talking about.

28. FLEXIBILITY

The Peace Corps encourages that their volunteers work on a secondary project within your community. You have almost full autonomy on the project based off of your experiences and what your community is in need of. There are also other Peace Corps projects that you can take advantage of like in my country there was PEPFAR which is the Presidents Emergency Plan for Aids Response. This required us to teach about AIDS and AID prevention. It allowed us to travel to other sites to teach these curriculums, and we were allowed to go to training for it in the Capital. In Ghana they had something similar but for malaria prevention which my friend who served in Ghana participated in. If interested take advantage of these opportunities, which I promise you will not regret doing so.

29. INTEGRATION.

Integrating into my community was very easy for me, my community embraced me with open arms. For other volunteers' integration which is an integral part of Peace Corps service wasn't as easy. I was lucky and had a really good service site and community, but despite that I recommend going with the flow, say yes as often as you can. Don't say no unless it's a mater of safety and security. Push yourself out of your comfort zone, and integration will come a lot easier. I was told by my friend if you only successfully integrated into your community you did a good job. Another thing is to figure out what the community does often together and participate in that. For example, tea is very important in Ukraine, and almost everyone bonded over tea so I would sit down with people and just have a cup of tea with them.

30. FRIENDSHIPS

Some of the friendships you make during your time in the Pace Corps could be the friendships that will last the longest. You have a shared experience so deep that its hard to break that connection and understanding that you all have, and these kinds of friendships can transcend distance. I am still in contact with many of the friends I made through out my Peace Corps service, and my friend who served in Ghana still contacts his Peace Corps friends on a regular basis. The memories you all will share are priceless and I have a feeling you will not take them for granted. Do your best to stay in contact through out your service and once you return state side as well.

31. MAKING SMALL DIFFERENCES

One of the things that many of the Peace Corps volunteers struggle with is the fact that they are only making a small difference. Many of the Peace Corps volunteers that enter service have an idea of making a big change but let's be honest that isn't going to happen. More likely the biggest change that is going to happen is in the way you see the world and how you view yourself which is a great added benefit of Peace Corps service. Do not let this dissuade you from service, although you will not be making a big difference you are making a difference in the community in which you are serving which is monumental for that community. You are impacting a lot of lives, even though it might not be as many as you had originally hoped. Do not also get disheartened by this fact as well, do you best and watch the impact you make o nyour community.

32. CONVERSIONS

The one thing about America and dealing with other countries is that most of the world deals with the metric system. Most countries use meters instead of miles, Celsius instead of Fahrenheit and so on. Science and math classes were a long time ago and I know I had a hard time with the conversions at first. My recommendation is that you find a good app and download it on your smart phone. I did this and it was a life saver, plus with the weather, the app on my phone allowed you to switch the temperature from Fahrenheit to Celsius which I used the most. Also if you plan to bake or cook bring your own set of measuring cups, it will make the process so much easier, at that point you will not have to convert anything if you follow basic American recipes like I do.

33. NAVIGATING GENDER AND SOCIETAL ROLES AND NORMS

Male and Female alike have there on separate challenges when dealing with the gender and social roles of there given countries. For me one of the gender roles I succumbed to a lot was living alone. Many people in my community thought I was brave for living on my own as a woman, because most women live with their parents until they get married and build their own house. AS I was preparing to move out of my host house, I would constantly get asked whether or not I am scared that boys might come knocking on my door in the middle of the night. I shrugged and told them not really. The reverse of this was when I herd a male Peace Corps Volunteer talk about how his Host Family asked who was going to cook for him and do his laundry when he moved out. The short answer, he was of course but to most

Ukrainians, that was seen as a woman's task. My recommendation is to be as independent as possible and show them that things are different in America, in as nice of a way as possible. Use this opportunity to share your culture and customs as well.

34. REPORTING

Just like any government project paperwork is very important which is why it shouldn't be that much of a surprise to find out that yes you will have to write reports. The reports can be lengthy, but they only happen once or twice a year, so in all honesty it really isn't that bad. The one way to make reporting time come easier for you though is to keep a log of your activities related to your Peace Corps work. This includes what took place, how long was spent on the project and when. It would also be important to note who participated in the project as well. Be as detailed as possible when taking notes. I also recommend using a calendar to keep track of all the dates you did something, so you are not just guessing when you create your report.

35. ACRONYMS

You could probably tell by all the acronyms that I have already dropped that the Peace Corps has a fondness for Acronyms and uses them whenever possible. Some of the Acronyms include RPCV, or PCV which stands for Returned Peace Corps Volunteer and Peace Corps Volunteer. Some of the others are PCMO Peace Corps Medical Office, and HCN Home Country National. During training you will also have an LCF Language and Culture Facilitator and a TCF Technical and Cultural Facilitator. These people will be HCN. Don't worry about trying to memorize all the acronyms you will hear them a lot and it will not take you long to catch on.

36. PERSONAL SPACE

In many places the concept of personal space is very different than our own. Many countries vary in this, all I can speak in this matter really is my personal experience. In Ukraine there are times when having your personal space invaded is common. For one my host parents had no problem just walking into my room when I kept the door open, which I normally did for that reason. I wanted to make a good impression on my host family and be as welcoming as they were. There were also times when riding a taxi to the nearest town that many people were all squished in at once. This can happen as well. Just be careful and do what makes you feel comfortable and try and be understanding of your host family's culture and customs.

37. LANGUAGE BARRIERS

Many parts of Peace Corps Service is hard, some harder than most, but one of the most challenging thing is dealing with the language barrier. When I arrived in Ukraine I knew nothing about the language, but I was quickly taught enough to get by on most occasions. Do your best to learn the language but it is ok if you don't catch on as fast as you'd like. In the meantime, try communicating with some gestures and its okay to ask for help by a member of the Peace Corps staff especially at the beginning. You will have Host Country Nationals during training that will help you communicate with your Host Family in the beginning and this person will probably be your language teacher.

38. MONEY

No matter the country you go to the money is probably going to be different than in the United States. For example, in Ukraine the money was called hryvna and back then it was worth roughly 28 to the dollar. Money while in Ukraine seemed to be able to go a longer way than it would have in America. That being said I highly recommended buying things based off of what you make and how much they cost in the country you live in. If you base your purchases off of what it would cost you in the States you will go broke pretty fast. Budget based off of what Peace Corps gives you, and don't worry so much about the price comparison. Secondly, I want to talk about finances in America. I think it is a good idea to have someone you trust be able to access your bank account on your behalf. Also, I did not do this, and I didn't know, but check with your bank and make sure you'd still be able to access your bank account online from where you are going. I was not able to view my bank account and it put me in a really bad position.

39. IT'S ALL ABOUT THE SMALL THINGS IN LIFE

One thing I noticed in coming back to the States after my service is how much my I missed some of the small things in life. I guess I kind of realized this back in the country when I was feeling homesick, but it really came into focus For one thing, Peanut butter was a huge thing I missed, which I didn't know was a very uncommon thing in a lot of countries. My friend told me a story about hist time in Ghana, and how he once was sent a package of cheese which was hard to get in his country. He told me at the time he felt like the cheese king, which is kind of funny to think how something so small like cheese can make your day. I recommend doing your best and enjoy the small things when you can during service, it will do so much good to your mental health.

40. THIRD WORLD PROBLEMS

One thing you'll have to get use to is dealing with third world or should I say first word problems. Cold water sometimes, lack of internet, maybe cooking over a fire or gas stove, and using a match to light it. I would take this into account when planning your service. I personally lived in area where I had some modern luxuries like running hot water, but that is not always going to be the case. Camping is a good example of what it is like to live in a third world country, but not a whole picture. Just be prepared for the worst and you'll be ecstatic when the best happens.

41. OVERWHELMING

Oftentimes service and the time that follows can be overwhelming, a lot is happening, and a lot is changing both in your surroundings and the way you view the world. I say both because returning back to the United States after service can be an adjustment as well Try journaling your thoughts or making a list when things are getting tough. Any positive coping mechanism you have will be just as good as well. Also do not be afraid to ask for help, there is a whole community out there that has experienced the same things you ha6ve, use them if you want. Also, going into your service you will be required to fill out a lot of paperwork for many different things. There is a lot of paperwork and that for me was very overwhelming, with that I suggest taking it one day at a time.

42. HOLIDAYS

Holidays can be the times when you will feel the most homesick, especially if you live in a country that doesn't celebrate all the Holidays the way that you do. There is also a flipside to this phenomenon when you celebrate the holidays specific to your host country. It fosters inclusivity and makes you feel welcomed and appreciated. I recommend participating in these holidays and customs any chance you get. Plus, you don't have to be alone on American holidays either. Make plans to spend time with fellow PCV's or use this opportunity to share this holiday with your host community. I know for Thanksgiving I made a thanksgiving meal for my host family and shared it with them and their extended family. It was a blast and really helped me not to feel lonely on the Holidays.

43. TALK TO A RECRUITER BEFORE LEAVING

If you have any real logistical questions before you leave or while you consider whether or not the Peace Corps is the right fit for you. I suggest talking to a recruiter. A recruiter can help guide you in the right direction and can answer many questions you have or lead you in the right direction. There is also the added benefit that most if not all recruiters have served in the Peace Corps at one point in their life, most PC corporate staff have spent time as a Peace Corps Volunteer as well so they can share their experience with you. Do not be afraid to ask questions, they are there to help you.

44. EVERYONE'S SERVICE IS DIFFERENCE 6

Perhaps if you take nothing away but one thing from everything, I have written this far it would be this point. Remember no one service is going to be the same, you may feel disappointed if you try and compare yours to others. For one thing a Volunteer may not do a lot in terms of projects or visiting other

PCV's and hosting seminars or whatnot, but they may have integrated into their Host Community really well. Everyone is different, everyone has different talents, so please I beg you do not compare your service to others! You will do great in whatever you do at site and that is all that matters at the end of the day.

45. SENSE OF PURPOSE

One thing many of the other RPCV's that I have talked to mentioned was that they felt a sense of purpose during there service and felt that what they were doing something meaningful. Peace Corps service can be very meaningful and can give you a sense of purpose you may have been lacking. This sense of purpose can carry you on through the rest of your life in everything you do. Peace Corps Service shows that no matter how small the task may be, that task can be meaningful.

46. CHANGE OF PERSPECTIVE

Peace Corps service can change the way you view the world in many different aspects. First of all, like I mentioned earlier, Peace Corps service can make you appreciate the small things a whole lot more. Secondly serving in the Peace Corps can teach you to be more tolerant of the people around you, and more understanding of there situation. It will change the way you view other interactions and how other countries interact as well. These are all good things to learn, and I think they are a highly appreciated asset that employers gain from hiring Returned Peace Corps Volunteers. Another change I think is you value the time spent with your family. I know that in Ukraine family was taken in very high regard and I learned a lot from there sense of family and was able o bring it into my own life.

47. OPPORTUNITIES

The Peace Corps opens the door to so many different opportunities, which was one of the reasons why I joined the peace corps. However, there are a lot of opportunities for learning and growth that take place during your Peace Corps service as well. Like I mentioned there are training opportunities that give you the chance to do more than what you're a just assigned to do. Plus one thing I haven't mentioned is that during your service you are allowed and paid to hire a language tutor so you can keep studying and learning the language of your host country. Once you completed your service, Peace Corps often hosts a work fair that you can attend. This work fair allows you to talk to many different people who are hiring and allows you to make a good impression. Look into the opportunities that the Peace Corps provides, they could be beneficial for your service and for your future.

48. EVACUATION

No one goes into their term of service thinking that at some point they will get evacuated. When evacuation happens, it is hard on everyone, yourself, the community that you served and the other Peace Corps staff in country. In the past year no one would predict that there would be a world-wide evacuation of all Peace Corps volunteers due to Covid-19, but it happened. I remembered coming home after that completely devastated, it is hard and is still hard a little over a year later. Evacuation is part of the emergency action plan that the safety and security team had in place, and it works in different stages.

First you are put on alert and told to stay home, and if you aren't home, to go get there ASAP. When I got this message, we all knew that Evacuation was inevitable. The safety and Security team will send you updates until the final decision has been made and the evacuation process is started. If this ever happens to you and you end up being Evacuated know you are not alone. Know it is ok to cry and to hurt and try to look on the bright side.

49. NON-COMPETITIVE ELIGIBILITY

One of the benefits of Peace Corps service is that you get non-competitive eligibility on government position. Now non-competitive eligibility can be kind of confusing, and it doesn't mean that you will automatically get what ever job you apply for, but it will put you at the top of the list. Make sure to use this if you can and don't just let it fade out. That being said being a Peace Corps volunteer in and of itself can get you a lot of credit when applying for jobs so make sure that you add it to your resume as soon as you can. You will also be able to receive a scholarship of sorts to many different schools out there if accepted which is always great if you are looking to further your education.

50. REINTEGRATION

What happens when your service ends? Well, you go back to America where you have to reintegrate into American society all over again. Now this may seem very easy, but it really isn't, at least for me it wasn't easy at all. To me it felt like reintegrating back into America was harder than integrating into the host country I was sent to. Though to be fair I was sent home in the middle of a Pandemic which was rough for everybody. That being said I wasn't alone, and I had my family to surround me. My advice for you when it is time for you to come back to America spend time with Family and Friends as much as possible.

OTHER RESOURCES:

One of the helpful resources online can be through blogs, these tend to be country specific but are good to read when preparing to leave for your country of service.

Youtube can also be a huge source of information with vlogs and the sort on it so it would hurt researching there as well. Be skeptical though what you read on blogs and vlogs because they are told by a singulars persons point of view and like I said everyone service is different.

Another helpful resource I found was reddit, this platform has a lot of PCV, RPCV, and others on it. Here you can ask questions, or search for a specific question because most likely it has already been asked. https://www.reddit.com

Another beneficial site I found was the actual Peace Corps Website, here you can find a lot of information in many different sectors. www.peacecorps,gov

The last place I would recommend going to if you want more information on the exact country you are going to would be the CIA world factbook. This website has a treasure trove of information https://www.cia.gov/the-world-factbook

READ OTHER 50 THINGS TO KNOW BOOKS

50 Things to Know About Coping With Stress: By A Mental Health Specialist by Kimberly L. Brownridge

50 Things to Know About Being a Zookeeper: Life of a Zookeeper by Stephanie Fowlie

50 Things to Know About Becoming a Doctor: The Journey from Medical School of the Medical Profession by Tong Liu MD

50 Things to Know About Knitting: Knit, Purl, Tricks & Shortcuts by Christina Fanelli

50 Things to Know

Stay up to date with new releases on Amazon:

https://amzn.to/2VPNGr7

CZYKPublishing.com

50 Things to Know

We'd love to hear what you think about our content! Please leave your honest review of this book on Amazon and Goodreads. We appreciate your positive and constructive feedback. Thank you.

www.ingramcontent.com/pod-product-compliance
Lightning Source LLC
Chambersburg PA
CBHW070317220526
45465CB00004B/1886